Doris Salcedo
Shibboleth

Shibboleth is a negative space:
it addresses the w(hole) in history
that marks the bottomless
difference that separates whites
from non-whites. The w(hole) in
history that I am referring to is
the history of racism, which runs
parallel to the history of modernity,
and is its untold dark side.

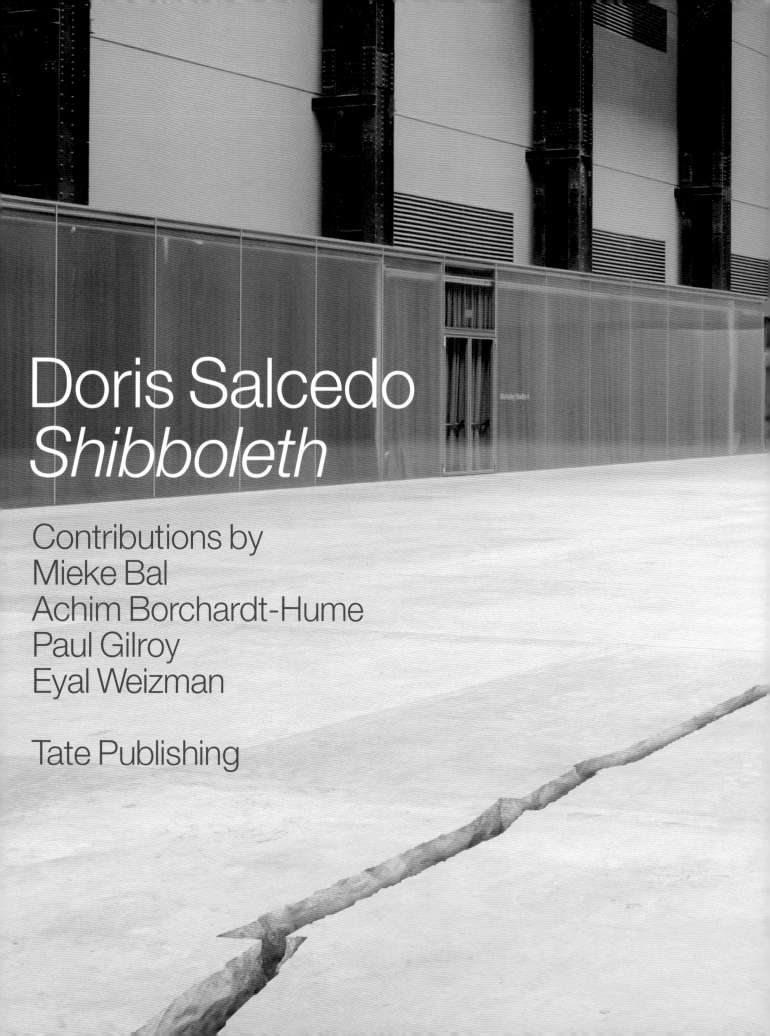

Doris Salcedo
Shibboleth

Contributions by
Mieke Bal
Achim Borchardt-Hume
Paul Gilroy
Eyal Weizman

Tate Publishing

The Unilever Series
An Annual art commission sponsored by Unilever

Unilever

Published by order of the Tate Trustees on the
occasion of the exhibition at Tate Modern, London
9 October 2007 – 6 April 2008

This exhibition is the eighth commission
in The Unilever Series

Published in 2007 by Tate Publishing,
a division of Tate Enterprises Ltd,
Millbank, London SW1P 4RG
www.tate.org.uk/publishing

© Tate 2007

British Library Cataloguing in Publication Data
A catalogue record for this book is available from
the British Library

ISBN 978-1-85437-719-7

Designed by Rose
Printed by BAS Printers, Romsey

Measurements of artworks are given in
centimetres, height before width

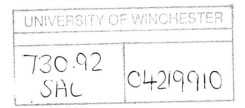

Contents

Sponsor's Foreword

It is a source of great pride to all of us at Unilever that for the last eight years we have been able to help bring some of the world's greatest artists to the unique setting of Tate Modern's Turbine Hall. So far over 17 million people from the UK and around the world have been able to view and experience some truly remarkable installations.

This year we are delighted to welcome Doris Salcedo, whose installation *Shibboleth* continues the tradition of innovation and experimentation established by previous artists in The Unilever Series.

Like all great artists Salcedo invites us to see the world differently. She asks us to reflect on the boundaries – physical and emotional – that divide us as human beings.

This is an exploration that resonates within Unilever. Understanding patterns of human behaviour is vital to a company that strives to meet consumers' everyday needs with products that make people feel good, look good and get more out of life.

As a founder sponsor of Tate Modern, Unilever is proud to have helped make inspirational contemporary art accessible to so many people through The Unilever Series.

We hope you will be moved by Doris Salcedo's work.

Patrick Cescau
Group Chief Executive, Unilever plc

Director's Foreword

Since Tate Modern opened in 2000, the Turbine Hall has become one of the most iconic art spaces worldwide. Forming a transitional area between the streets of Southwark and the museum galleries it has also become one of the most popular public spaces in London. Apart from its architectural monumentality it is this dual dimension of art and the public sphere which makes it a unique environment – and challenge – for any artist to work in. Doris Salcedo fully rose to this challenge when, much to our delight, she accepted our invitation to conceive the eighth commission in The Unilever Series.

Tate's relationship with Salcedo dates back almost a decade. In 1999 the artist presented her critically acclaimed sculptural installation *Unland* as part of the then Tate Gallery's *Art Now* series. Like so much of Salcedo's art, these three sculptures, made from precariously conjoined domestic tables with their surfaces painstakingly covered with cloth and weaves of human hair, quietly bore witness to the pain and grief of those exposed to violence. Tate was fortunate to be able to acquire one of these powerful works, *Unland, audible in the mouth* (1998) for its collection where it was subsequently joined by two *Untitled* sculptures.

For the past five years Salcedo's work has increasingly addressed the public sphere. In 2002 she lowered 280 chairs from the roof of the Palace of Justice in Colombia's capital Bogotá, paying homage to those killed there in a failed guerrilla coup seventeen years earlier. Blurring the lines between performance and sculpture this extraordinary action publicly confronted memories of this traumatic event for the first time. The following year, at the Istanbul Biennial 2003, she filled a derelict housing plot with 1,550 wooden chairs to evoke the extreme experience of war. More recently, she shrouded the white-washed walls of a sun-flooded gallery in the historic Castello di Rivoli, Turin, with a brick skin, seemingly suspended from the room's brick vault. By blind-folding the castle's representative architecture, Salcedo created a vivid memorial to those excluded from systems of power, past and present.

Shibboleth expands on Salcedo's previous preoccupations by challenging the predominant Western-centric understanding of modernity. The installation reminds us that the history of colonialism and racism is the Janus-face of the history of Enlightenment and the strife towards a Utopian world-order. This reminder could not be more timely as Tate is seeking to revaluate its historic mission to collect 'international' modern art on behalf of the nation. To look towards the future we need to face the past. The importance of artists such as Doris Salcedo and their insistence that the histories of the 'one' and the 'other' are one and the same cannot be overestimated in this context.

Rather than fill the cavernous volume of the Turbine Hall, Salcedo proposed to inscribe a negative space into its floor. *Shibboleth* is thus not just a metaphorical but an actual transformation of Tate Modern and one that we feel will have an impact far beyond the physical and temporal confines of the commission. I would like to take this opportunity to express my heartfelt gratitude to Doris Salcedo for conceiving such an extraordinary project for Tate Modern and for realising it with such courage and determination.

In this she was supported by her team of architects and technicians who have worked tirelessly on the many aspects of this project from its inception through to the final installation. We would like to thank particularly Sergio Clavijo, Fredy Florez, Carlos Granada, Pia Mazzilli and Joaquín Sanabria for their warm collaboration as well as William Ahumada, Alfonso Amaya, Edwin Amaya, Annabelle Beauchamp, Jovanny Becerra, Luis Beltrans, Manuel Campos, Andrea Cano, Dario Cardenas, Marino Castaño, Wbaldo Castaño, Oscar Castillo, Yul Hans Castillo, German Cunides, John Freddy Galvis, Wilson Galvis, Luis Gonzaga, Jorge Lopes, Juan Camilo Meja, Jesus Molina, Javier Monroy, Jonathan Monroy, Juana Montoya, Marco Murcia, Andrea Navas, Daniel Panqueva, Juan Carlos Pedraza, Olga Perez, Jose Peralta, Ancizar Rincón, Edilson Rios, Efrain Rojas, Jose Edisson Rumique, Oscar Sanabria, Diego Suarez, Roberto Uribe, Carlos Andres Vargas and Ramón Villamarín. In our gratitude we also include Azriel Bibliowicz.

At Tate Modern, Achim Borchardt-Hume, Curator, Modern and Contemporary Art has curated and managed the project with great dedication and professionalism, his unwavering enthusiasm helping to overcome even the most challenging moments. Ben Borthwick, Assistant Curator, Tate Modern has provided invaluable organisational support.

Our efforts have been greatly augmented by the unstinting help of Salcedo's galleries. At Alexander and Bonin in New York we thank Carolyn Alexander and Ted Bonin and at White Cube in London we thank Jay Jopling, Tim Marlow, Susan May and Daniela Gareh for their unceasing belief in the project. In addition we gratefully acknowledge the generous support of a number of private individuals.

Shibboleth posed a number of exceptional technical challenges which could only be overcome with the help of professionals recognised as leading experts in their field. Stuart Smith, Director, ARUP from the outset worked closely with Doris Salcedo and her team on solving the many engineering issues. In this he was ably supported by Richard Lawson, Engineer.

The process of installation was expertly planned and overseen by Dean Morelli, Project Director, and Roger Leach, Project Manager at Morgan Ashurst PLC and we thank James Breckon, Managing Director, Major Projects and Martin Broome, Managing Director for their support. The sensitivity with which the construction companies executed their part of the installation was vital for the final success of the project. We could not have entrusted this process to a better team than Gary Dann, Director, Mann Construction Ltd and Russell Pooley, Managing Director, and Martin Bull, Project Manager at Associated Stone Group, with additional thanks to Peter Sloane, Brick Image. Advice in the early stages of the project was provided by Paul Salmon, Joint Managing Director, Byrne Bros Ltd and Jim Mackey, Managing Director, McGee Group Ltd. We would also like to thank Peter Rogers, Director, Stanhope PLC for his helpful input at critical junctures.

The catalogue was edited by Achim Borchardt-Hume with view to forming a lasting record of the commission. We are extremely grateful to Paul Gilroy, Anthony Giddens Professor in Social Theory at the London School of Economics; Eyal Weizman, Director of the Centre for Research Architecture at Goldsmiths College and Mieke Bal, Academy Professor at the Royal Netherlands Academy of Arts and Sciences, for their insightful contributions. We would also like to thank Alice Chasey at Tate Publishing, and Simon Elliott and Terry Stephens at Rose for their creative design work.

Too many to mention, we thank all our colleagues at Tate, without whose boundless energy and passion for making art accessible to a wider public it would be impossible to realise a project of such complexity. Special thanks go to Stephen Mellor, Co-ordinator Exhibitions and Displays, and Phil Monk, Art Installation Manager, for facilitating the smooth collaboration between the various working teams. In addition we would like to acknowledge Sir Nicholas Serota, Director, Tate and Sheena Wagstaff, Chief Curator, Tate Modern for their involvement and support.

Finally, we are exceedingly grateful to Unilever for its continuous commitment to Tate Modern and for sponsoring this, the eighth commission in The Unilever Series. Without their significant support it would simply not be possible to undertake projects of this ambition and scale. Unilever have pledged ongoing support for the Series until 2012, guaranteeing Tate the opportunity to continue to present these unique and exceptional projects. For their steadfast vision and commitment to Tate we would like to offer their Group CEO Patrick Cescau, Senior Vice President, Global Corporate Responsibility Gavin Neath and UK Chairman Dave Lewis our most sincere thanks.

Vicente Todolí
Director, Tate Modern

Artist's Acknowledgements

I would like to thank the many people involved in making this project possible. I am deeply grateful to Nicholas Serota for his courage in welcoming a work like *Shibboleth* into Tate Modern – it really was an act of open-mindedness and it is hard to think of another museum or institution that would share this outlook. Thanks also to his colleagues at Tate, including Vicente Todolí, Achim Borchardt-Hume and Ben Borthwick, who in particular showed kindness when I most needed it.

I would like to express my appreciation to the many supporters of my work who have also helped make *Shibboleth* possible.

I am thankful to White Cube and Alexander and Bonin for their unwavering support throughout this challenging project. Jay Jopling and Carolyn Alexander have been a steadfast source of strength; their belief in my work has given me the possibility to make uncompromising pieces. I have engaged in stimulating dialogue with Tim Marlow and am grateful to him for his invaluable friendship, along with Daniela Gareh, Tina Carmichael and Susannah Hyman, for the particular energy they have put into helping make *Shibboleth* possible. Very special thanks to Susan May, who took this project on as her own; her thoughtfulness, commitment and strength were vital to the realization of *Shibboleth*.

I am indebted to my studio team; their dedication, creativity and solidarity are an essential part of *Shibboleth*. I am privileged to work with the architects Sergio Clavijo, Fredy Florez, Carlos Granada, Pia Mazzilli and Joaquín Sanabria. Their intelligence and generosity towards my work have turned it into a joint adventure. Thanks to Ramón Villamarín, Roberto Uribe and Juana Montoya for their stubborn and marvellous solidarity. I am grateful to William Ahumada, Alfonso Amaya, Edwin Amaya, Annabelle Beauchamp, Jovanny Becerra, Luis Beltrans, Manuel Campos, Andrea Cano, Dario Cardenas, Marino Castaño, Wbaldo Castaño, Oscar Castillo, Yul Hans Castillo, German Cunides, John Freddy Galvis, Wilson Galvis, Luis Gonzaga, Jorge Lopes, Juan Camilo Meja, Jesus Molina, Javier Monroy, Jonathan Monroy, Marco Murcia, Andrea Navas, Daniel Panqueva, Juan Carlos Pedraza, Olga Perez, Jose Peralta, Ancizar Rincón, Edilson Rios, Efrain Rojas, Jose Edisson Rumique, Oscar

Sanabria, Diego Suarez and Carlos Andres Vargas. I also thank Stuart Smith, Dean Morelli, Gary Dann, Martin Bull and Peter Sloane for helping turn *Shibboleth* into a reality.

Finally I would like to thank Azriel Bibliowicz whose tolerance and humour make not only my work but my life possible.

Doris Salcedo

Sculpting Critical Space
Achim Borchardt-Hume

The Senator:
This is an abyss into which it is better not to look.

The Count:
My friend, we are not free not to look.

Joseph de Maistre, St Petersburg Dialogues[1]

1
Joseph de Maistre, St Petersburg Dialogues, or Conversations on the Temporal Government of Providence, *translated by Richard A. Lebrun, Montreal and Kingston, London and Buffalo, McGill-Queen's University Press, 1993, p.145. I would like to acknowledge the use of the same epigraph by John Gray,* Black Mass: Apocalyptic Religion and the Death of Utopia, *London 2007.*

2
Patrick Hanks (ed.), Collins Dictionary of the English Language, *2nd ed., London and Glasgow 1986, p.1407.*

The carefully considered titles of Doris Salcedo's sculptural installations add an important layer of meaning to a body of work critically acclaimed for its sensitive use of materials and sophisticated deployment of scale. Alluding to a poem by the German-Jewish poet Paul Celan, she named her ensemble of three table sculptures at the New Museum, New York in 1998 *Unland*. Echoing the German *unheimlich*, subject of an essay by Sigmund Freud rather unsatisfactorily translated as 'the uncanny', the neologism *Unland* alluded to a geopolitical terrain defined by what it was not. Just as the prefix *un* turned the German *heim* – the home, with all its connotations of comfort and protection – into a place of fear and dread, Salcedo subverted the idea of land, with its implied sense of ownership and clearly defined boundaries, into its very opposite: the terrain of the dispossessed, of those who cannot lay claim to the physical and social territory of their existence. Similarly, the title of Salcedo's installation in the historic Castello di Rivoli, Turin in 2005, *Abyss*, made reference not to the claustrophobic brick enclosure created by the artist but to a vertiginous sense of falling. The post-colonial condition of being shut out, in and up – physically, intellectually and metaphorically – here was likened to a terrifying vertical drop.

The title of Salcedo's installation for Tate Modern's Turbine Hall, *Shibboleth*, commonly denotes 'a custom, phrase or use of language that acts as a test of belonging to, or as stumbling block to becoming a member of, a particular social class, profession, etc.'[2] Its meaning originates in an episode recounted in Chapter 12 of the *Book of Judges* describing the massacre of the Ephraimites at the hand of the Gileadites around 1370–1070 BC. According to the Old Testament narrative the Gileadites, having defeated the Ephraimites in battle, challenged any survivors seeking to cross the river Jordan to enunciate the word 'shibboleth'. The Ephraimites, unable to form the 'sh' sound

Unland
the orphan's tunic
1997
Wood, cloth, hair and glue
80 x 245 x 98
Caixa Forum, Barcelona

Abyss
Installation view, Triennial of Contemporary
Art, Castello di Rivoli, Turin
2005
Brick, cement, steel and epoxy resin
441 x 1386 x 1624

of the victors' language, pronounced the word 'sibboleth' instead, and in so doing spelt their own death sentence: forty-two thousand of them were killed, the single largest massacre recounted in the Bible. One of the peculiarities of the story is that the Ephraimites at the point of slaughter were no longer aggressors, but refugees desperately seeking to reach their homeland. Their slaughter was not a military necessity, but an early premonition that violence follows its own logic, which however much disputed by rationalist thought loses nothing of its terrifying forcefulness.

Bearing witness to those who have suffered the consequences of violence is a driving force that underpins much of Salcedo's oeuvre, and connects her early sculptures and gallery installations, such as the aforementioned *Unland* series, with the large-scale projects she has concentrated on over the past five years. Violence equals a breakdown of all other forms of communication. After all, the root cause of the battle between Gileadites and Ephraimites was the latters' feeling of having been wrongfully sidelined by their former allies. In this regard violence, over-determined with no room for constructive response, is the opposite to any generative act of communication, at the heart of which lies a critical space that is open to interpretation.

In the best possible scenario, this critical space is one that allows voices and thoughts to be heard that hitherto were silenced or remained unspoken. It is a space that demands trust and commitment, and that allows for going beyond the initial intention of the speaker. Salcedo generates such critical spaces by making works that, while informed by her political sensibility and her lived experience, not least the troublesome history of her native Colombia, refuse to be confined to any one reading; works that, while being the result of long, painstaking labour, denote a starting point rather than a finishing line. *Shibboleth* is the latest such work, actually and metaphorically opening a critical space that runs right through the heart of Tate Modern.

Museums and art galleries are repositories of history. Popularised in the nineteenth century, they are intimately connected to the ideology of nationhood and, as a result, deeply entangled in the Yin of Enlightenment, democracy and Utopian rationalism and the Yang of colonialism, racism and exclusion of 'the other'; even though much effort is being made to present art as unaffected by this dichotomy, following its own history, i.e. *art history*. In reality, Western-centric Modernism, which forms the backbone of Tate's collection of *international* modern art, as heir apparent to the Enlightenment tradition is intrinsically caught up in this dynamic, the white walls of the galleries it customarily inhabits demarcating not just aesthetically but also ideologically 'white space'. Much of the new cultural globalism, which all too often only thinly disguises late capitalism's

Gordon Matta-Clark
Splitting
1974
Chromogenic print mounted on board
101.6 x 76.2
Metropolitan Museum of Art

Hans Haacke
GERMANIA
1993
Installation for the German Pavilion,
Venice Biennale

need for ever-expanding markets as its driving force, does little genuinely to broaden this space, given that it leaves its ideological foundations intact. Instead, Salcedo cuts right through them.

The act of cutting is motivated in equal measure by anger and the will to harm as by a mode of doubt and enquiry, of 'testing the limits'. By creating a moment of disjuncture, cuts offer a means to find out what lies *beneath* the surface, as is demonstrated by some of the most evocative cuts in the history of twentieth-century art. In the years following World War II, the Argentine-Italian painter and sculptor Lucio Fontana, for example, began to puncture and slice the surface of his canvases to create a new 'spatial' art. What, however, if one reads his radical gesture not just as a formalist attempt to overcome the two-dimensional confines of his medium, but as a quest to probe the limits and continuous possibilities of painting after the corruption of all imagery, representative and abstract, through Fascist ideology? Throughout the 1970s the US artist Gordon Matta-Clark questioned architecture's hierarchical aspirations towards eternity and monumentality by cutting apertures into derelict buildings destined for destruction. In so doing he turned fixed structures into situations characterised by precariousness and instability. Similarly, at the 1993 Venice Biennale, the US-based German artist Hans Haacke exposed the complex historic and ideological layers hidden in a structure such as the German Pavilion, grandly rebuilt under Adolf Hitler to demonstrate Teutonic superiority in all matters spiritual and cultural, by lifting its floor and rearranging the broken slabs in a disturbing homage to Caspar David Friedrich's painting *Sea of Ice* (c. 1823–24), one of the icons of German Romanticism. Enquiry and

Lucio Fontana
Concetto Spaziale – Attersea
(Spatial Concept – Expectation)
1964–65
Tempera on canvas, laquered wood
146.1 x 114.3
Walker Art Center

testing boundaries, creating a situation of precariousness and instability, and the recovery of layers of a history tempting to forget so as not to jeopardise the status quo of the present moment, all form part of Salcedo's ambition for *Shibboleth* too.

However, the slowly evolving drama of the steadily widening crack is just a point of entry for Salcedo. Her opening up of the Turbine Hall floor is accompanied by a second gesture, the insertion of a disturbing cavity created by fusing nature (Colombian rock face), tireless labour (the concrete cast thereof produced in Salcedo's Bogotá studio) and a man-made means of control (the wire mesh embedded in the cast). Full of associative potential yet without actual precedent in the outside world, the walls of this cavity quietly insist on their unique materiality and command close attention by virtue of their endlessly reworked surface detail. By choosing to go underground, the direction of the abject, rather than to reach up into the heights of the Turbine Hall with their promise of elevation, Salcedo implicitly challenges the lofty claims to beauty and truth that underpin much

of the art on view on Bankside's upper floors, and instead reclaims a territory for those excluded from these unilateral ideals. The mapping of subterranean space as the psycho-spatial terrain of those suppressed and exploited by the forces of so-called progress has haunted the imagination of the beneficiaries of their exploitation from the onset of modernity; from the terrifying architectural vision of Giambattista Piranesi's *Carceri* (1745) to Emile Zola's 1873 novel focusing on the chaos of working-class Paris, aptly named *Le Ventre de Paris* (*The Belly of Paris*). The subterranean parameter running the length of *Shibboleth's* concrete innards, then, is also a reminder that the privileges of those born on the 'right' side of the fence inherently rely on the very same privileges being withheld from others.

However, *Shibboleth* represents a fault line that runs not just through an abstract ideological, but through a concrete urban space. The Turbine Hall, officially designated a covered street, separates the galleries on the north side of the building from the generators distributing electricity on the south, their gentle hum a constant reminder of the converted power station's industrial past. While visitors to the museum delight in the views across the river to the City of London, with its architect-designed high rises attesting to the financial prowess of their corporate owners, the windowless back of the building overlooks the less salubrious areas of South London, traditionally home to the immigrant communities whose contribution to this past goes widely unrecognised.

The Turbine Hall runs parallel to the Thames, London's historico-geographical shibboleth which for centuries separated the city of respectability from the 'other' side of the river, that of the poor and social misfits. With the south increasingly gentrified – not least due to the presence of Tate Modern – there remain countless invisible territories across London, a city obsessed with the rising value of real estate; territories that only momentarily attract the spotlight as the scenes of violence and crime, with the young and vulnerable increasingly the target. Echoing the wire fence of Salcedo's subterranean chasm, the diamond pattern in Chris Ofili's *No Woman No Cry* (1998), for instance – the painter's tribute to Stephen Lawrence, the investigation into whose senseless killing led to the recognition of institutionalised racism within the British police force – is a subtle reminder of the dividing lines (some material, some not) that continue to cut across our urban spaces and society.

While the Turbine Hall's monumentality feeds the hunger of a profane culture for sublime experiences, *Shibboleth* quietly refuses to be comfortably consumed – in fact it is impossible to survey the entire work from a single viewing position. Starting as a hairline crack at the West Entrance, the installation eventually disappears from sight underneath the eastern glass walls, seemingly endless – just as the

3
Jacques Rancière, On the Shores of Politics,
London 2007, p. 29.

4
Ibid, p. 36.

questions it asks are open-ended. To experience the work, visitors have to commit the time it takes to walk its 150-metre length, the concrete void steadily drawing their gaze downwards. Akin to a procession, this walk invites us to look at what we have been conditioned to look away from, and to recognise the limitations of the humanist ideals at the heart of Western art and culture. This recognition is a difficult and painful one. As the French philosopher Jacques Rancière wrote:

'In the terror of the century, philosophy refuses to acknowledge any principle but its own original error: the old but ever-young betrayal called metaphysics, which abandons the task of illuminating what is in the imperilled light of being, and instead sets up an all-powerful subject presiding over a world of objects placed at its disposal; this principle of the omnipotence of the subject and of the devastation of the world fulfils itself in the reign of technology, while the political terror it exerts appears as just one of its achievements (the corpses in the gas chamber, certainly, but also the land laid waste by agribusiness, and so forth).'[3]

Rancière goes on to define as philosophy's most pressing business what equally may be defined as art's most pressing task in a world increasingly torn apart by intolerance and violence: 'how to deal with fear and hate.'[4]

For six months, *Shibboleth* opens a critical space for engagement with these difficult issues. Thereafter, a scar in the Turbine Hall's concrete floor will be all that will remain. *Shibboleth* will be gone. Tate Modern, however, will never be the same again.

Brokenness, Division and the Moral Topography of Post-Colonial Worlds
Paul Gilroy

In the Spanish world, and later in the European world in general, it fell to the warrior to establish domination over others. The conquistador was the first modern, active, practical human being to impose his violent individuality on the Other.

Enrique Dussel

1
Aimé Césaire, Discourse On Colonialism
trans. Joan Pinkham, Monthly Review books, 1972.

By now, the idea that our world is broken ought to be familiar. It corresponds directly to the ambivalent history of modernity as both progress and catastrophe. That duality was especially evident in the modernising dynamics of empire and colony. It shaped the formative encounters between Europe and the extra-historical parts of the world that supplied its wealth, paving the way to planetary domination. Now, observed from a contemporary, European vantage point, the same brokenness communicates the lingering impact of unresolved encounters between the horrors of the twentieth century and the modernist creativity which struggled to answer those events without the consolation of theodicy.

The civilising power of art salved the disillusion of Europe's cosmopolitans and helped them through the trauma of the 1914–18 war. Genocide, transposed from the tropics to the metropole, opened the same cultural traditions to accusations of complicity with cruelty and useless violence. Industrialised mass killing had been rationally applied as a mode of government. The murderous techniques that had emerged from colonial warfare effectively reshaped Europe's political, moral and cultural landscape around the eugenic imperatives of ultra-nationalism and racial hygiene.

Aimé Césaire's postwar essay, 'Discourse On Colonialism'[1] delivered an indictment of the West's civilisational bankruptcy. His prescient commentary was notable for being articulated on a world scale. It was spoken bitterly in the name of the stubborn majority of people dismissed by Europe and its various offshoots as infrahuman pagans and savages. The dream that art could have a special role in repairing this cultural and moral damage was renounced as inadequate.

Europe's past crimes and continuing pathologies were confirmed by its enduring attachments to the racial ordering of human life.

In those bleak circumstances, the pursuit of art, which was itself as broken as the wounded world, promised alternative possibilities as well as sources of hope.

With this critical counter-history of modern civilisation in mind, Doris Salcedo's work for the Turbine Hall returns us to a painful sense of our world's damaged character. That discomfort is connected to the agency of culture in securing division and hierarchy. This unsettling fissure is named *Shibboleth*. The ancient proper name refers to a combined process of admission and exclusion, to a cultural and linguistic test that brings either death or security. The test towards which she directs us is a variety of selection that relies on cultural mechanisms. Initially, it was the victors' means of determining who could and could not belong to their purified political and cultural community. The whole procedure gains additional power by being conducted close to killing.

The trial of identity conjured up here manifests the deepening divisions which increasingly define our damaged world. The naming of *Shibboleth* suggests the timelessness of this encounter with otherness, but the installation's timely execution fixes these problems firmly in our own era, where a similar deadly border will soon run through every social space and institution. Who is inside and who must stay outside will not only be determined at the airport or the frontier wire. Those fateful decisions will be made and repeated everywhere. They are now a central part of what our governments imagine security to be.

The Martiniquean revolutionary, Frantz Fanon, is remembered not so much for his adaptation of a militant anti-Nazi morality to the anti-colonial struggle, but for his still shocking view of colonial societies and his affirmative attitude to the insurrectionary movements that arose everywhere to overthrow them. Perhaps it helps to recall that Fanon was a healer as well as a warrior. His insights can help us now that our cities are hosting forms of segregation reminiscent of colonial conditions and now that other dismal innovations drawn from colonial laboratories are once again being imported into life behind the heavily fortified walls of resurgent, imperial overdevelopment.

Fanon had been a beneficiary of the best education the French Caribbean colonisers could provide. He was taught by Césaire at Lycée Schoelcher. Later, he studied in France, and qualified as a psychiatrist. As a decorated veteran of the anti-Nazi war, Fanon argued that, in colonial settings, the brokenness of European modernity had achieved uniquely destructive and damaging forms. An already unjust world was profoundly corrupted by its absolute reliance upon the Manichean divisions for which 'race' was emblematic. The violent situation that resulted not only made politics

2
Frantz Fanon Wretched of The Earth, *trans.
Constance Farrington, London 1967, p.29.*

impossible, but was psychologically and experientially toxic to its beneficiaries as well as to its victims. It alienated both settler and native, and damaged the torturer as well as the tortured. The different forms of human injury experienced by those shifting, open groups can be said, in a complex way, to have been complementary.

Fanon's uncomfortable insights become relevant here because he insisted that the motionless, social order of the colony was firmly and comprehensively compartmentalised: 'If we examine closely this system of compartments, we will at least be able to reveal the lines of force it implies … The colonial world is cut in two. The dividing line, the frontiers are shown by barracks and police stations … the policeman and the soldier are the official, instituted go-betweens.'[2] The dissident psychiatrist concluded by making explicit his central point about the relationship of power to law and space in the colonial city: 'This world cut in two is inhabited by two different species.'

In a post-colonial environment, which is busy reproducing some of the distinctive social and economic features that distinguished its colonial predecessor, Fanon's words suggest that the dividing line now cuts through the spaces of art and culture. These are also some of the places where the detachment and complicity of a public that routinely dwells in denial might be challenged. In other words, the gallery and museum can be made to host and to reveal the fundamental fissure that divides citizens from denizens and distinguishes the human from the infrahuman. By dramatising this fundamental cut and bringing it into the public space of quiet reflection, Salcedo exposes the divisions we prefer to ignore. She seems to suggest that the different species of which Fanon spoke can now make contact in the museum and the gallery as well as on the torturers' table.

It is worth emphasising that this view of Manichean division is not an endorsement of the 'clash of civilisations' idea. The contending forces are not just different versions of the same essential elements and attachments. The conflict between them is asymmetrical. The dividing lines are not straight. Power flows in varying configurations on different scales. Divisions, always marked by violence, move through – as well as between – the dubious civilisations which produce culture in order to draw the fatal line.

Securitocracy and info-war have made this a battle without an ending. Colonial government and immigration law provided an initial toolkit for managing the supposedly exceptional arrangements that suspend legality in legality's name. The new drama begins when the prisoners have been taken. Particularly if they resemble their captors, they will be subjected to the clarifying tests required by the victors' security. The racism that previously warranted exercises of this type no longer operates in the same obvious ways. Nowadays, what the political theorist Mahmood Mamdani calls 'culture-talk'[3] provides the novel medium in which these decisions are made legitimate.

Unlike Britain, Colombia, where Salcedo is based, cannot easily avoid the implications of its corrosive colonial history. That post-colonial society is premised upon the abiding ambivalence of the colonial period. The after-effects of brutal conquest remain a painful residue suspended in the everyday. The exploitation of nature and native alike supply a shameful, volatile history, especially where the accusing faces of indigenous peoples appear intact and articulate. Continuing civil war, narco-governance and narco-economy all feed enduring doubts about the losses involved in the transition to modernity and what Jean-Jacques Rousseau long ago identified as the 'fatal ingenuity' of the civilising process. In Latin America, post-colonial life supplies an invitation to mourn the losses involved in subjugation and to imagine what another, less belligerent developmental journey might have involved.

Colombia's geo-body is not a flat outline. It is a complex construction which is also endowed with depth. The country has created an elaborate and refined imaginative landscape that accentuates the difference between its various ecologies: the forested, tropical zones of the torrid areas and the colder, damp, cloudy world of its mountainous regions. Those ecologies don't exist on the same plane. They are arranged spatially so that one is found above the other. Their relationship complicates the routine topology characteristic of colonial life in which the wealthy opt for and defend the high ground. Colombia seems to have developed a special sensitivity to the relative height of different modes of dwelling which has been conducted into the core of national identity. The country lacked the extraordinary system of paved roads that was a feature of the old Inca empire and facilitated the Spanish conquest. The mountainous environment presented difficulties even to sure-footed mules. The difficulties involved in transit meant that for long periods, the only means to move between the climatically and symbolically different worlds that composed the nation was to be carried up and down the forbidding contours by another person, an indigenous *Sillero*, in an act of enforced intimacy. Michael Taussig has explored some of the consequences of this form of carriage, which, in the Colombian case, sharply alters the moral meaning of descent and ascent and produces the abyss as a limit against which the relative value of racialised life is to be determined.[4]

Compartmentalisation requires walls, fences, wire and gates. The pursuit of security may even have made the topography of the colonial world essentially vertical. Beneath the post- and neo-colonial streets of Latin America we can sometimes discover a second city. The vulnerable may even congregate there at night to

Above:
Precipitous Descent of a Cordillera of the Andes in the Province of Choco
Frontispiece to *Journal of a Residence and Travels in Colombia during the Years of 1823 and 1824*, volume 2, Charles Stuart Cochrane, London 1825
Bodleian Library, University of Oxford, 25.401 v.2

3
Mahmood Mamdani Good Muslim, Bad Muslim America, The Cold War and The Roots of Terror, *New York 2004.*

4
Michael Taussig Shamanism, Colonialism and The Wild Man: A Study in Terror and Healing, *Chicago 1987, Chapter 18.*

protect themselves. Perhaps they have opened up the concrete ground and climbed down into it seeking sanctuary. *Shibboleth* suggests that downward journey and discovers value in exposing the dubious foundations on which our doomed securitocracy has come to rest. Salcedo's art makes its troubling infrastructure visible. That modern innovation, the wire fence, can be revealed in and produced from the damaged substructure of cultural institutions that are not as innocent as they might wish or seem to be. The misunderstandings that have arisen from Tate's historic association with sugar provide a small instance of what this buried history can accomplish.

Salcedo's widening fissure produces a sense of depth as well as separation. Nothing appears to emerge from it except a new and unsettling understanding of the precarious fortification which separates our reflection from the primal vulnerability that is its unacknowledged precondition. In the crack, we glimpse the permeable barrier of security, buried and thus willfully consigned to the past. By looking down, we are not only confronting the foundations of our present, we seem to be digging up the history of our future in a daring act of anticipatory archaeology. This realignment of past and future speaks to the prospect of healing and, in the longer term, to the possibility of encounters with alterity that do not involve fear and anxiety alone.

As it did for Fanon, the intractable effects of division can only be answered with a morally acute return to the idea of humanity – reconceptualised on a worldly scale in an explicit opposition to the idea that racial hierarchies and ethnic divisions are absolute. *Shibboleth* suggests something else as well. It endorses the proposition that institutions like the museum and the gallery will have to be damaged if they are going to be adequate to the task of managing the relationship with otherness, with difference. Damaging those institutions is now an affirmative procedure. It can be productive. Hopefully, the effects of that encounter will endure even if they are superficially repaired. After all, it is not merely a matter of showing what lies beneath our feet, of exposing the silent underpinning of the impossible security that we are becoming inclined to take for granted. The fabric of the building has been damaged not only as a symbol of the broken world in need of repair, but as an acknowledgement of the material fact of its contested global existence.

The crack gets wider, and will go on getting wider. It opens our world on to another axis, and in our principled response to that reorientation lies the healing possibility of mourning and reconciliation. In that belated gesture, a deeper security than the variety proffered by military planners is waiting to be embraced.

Seismic Archaeology
Eyal Weizman

A crack is not a static state but a stage in a process of gradual shear that might expand and tear through a building's structure and skin along the line of least resistance. Cracks register the evolving contradictions between the static inertia of built structure and the constantly transforming field of forces operating around and within it. Cracks are thus both lines in space and processes in time. The crack through the floor of Tate Modern's Turbine Hall seems to respond to violent subterranean forces that stir underneath its surface. At the point when we confront it, it has already cut through the floor, splitting its surface in disoriented movement, yet another moment and it threatens to expand and cut furiously through the Tate's galleries and walls and spill out onto Bankside and beyond. In a sequence of cumulative failures, buildings would collapse into their footprints, but the crack – the abstract product of forces beyond design or signification – would remain, outliving the structures through which it tore, their symbolic and functional orders. Every built structure (to paraphrase Virilio) is the possibility of a new disaster. To build is thus also to construct infinite lines of destruction.

The fractured floor of the Tate resonates with increasingly ubiquitous images of destroyed and damaged buildings. The diffused set of ghostly conflicts colloquially known as the 'War on Terror' has brought violence into the heart of cities, turning buildings into potential targets and protected fortresses. War brings out the totemic quality of buildings. Bombs do not only affect the immediate site of their impact; rather, they send powerful shock waves travelling though the ground underneath their surface layer. The ground liquefies as it becomes the medium of forces.

When occurring in inhabited areas, seismic or man-made cracks cut large cross-sections through architectural, archaeological and geological strata. In the wake of these forms of destruction, surfaces are revealed as deep volumes, and hidden layers otherwise buried within the depth of materials and the ground are exposed to view. The practice of archaeology has one of its origins in the examination of historical data made visible by seismic cracks. Stacked layers of histories, lives, wars and destruction lie compacted by soil and by stone. As soon as archaeology was inaugurated as a distinct discipline, however, stratigraphy – the recording, reading and narration of the exposed palimpsest of historical layers – assumed a political dimension. The power of archaeology manifested itself in its ability to emphasise some pasts over others, to short-circuit or even block alternative histories from surfacing. The practices of archaeology were used to construct and support national and religious myths as well as territorial claims.

The crack in the floor of the Turbine Hall does not expose the layers of concrete, insulation and foundation that make up the floor of the Tate, nor the mud of the river bank that lies underneath it.[1] It reveals a crafted texture – a concrete cast of rock formation, monochromatic and desert-like, in which a chain-link wire fence is in some places embedded and in others visibly protruding. It is through this act of cracking and the revelation of the material composition within it that Doris Salcedo attempts to read a counter-archaeology of the building and the history to which it is networked. She claims that the negative space of the crack exposes a 'colonial and imperial history [that] has been disregarded, marginalised or simply obliterated …

1
One of the best decisions that architects Herzog & de Meuron took in transforming Bankside power station into Tate Modern was the excavation of the original floor level of the building, which originally stood at the level of the upper entrance. They removed this floor to place visitors on the lowest possible level, which is, in fact, under the water level of the Thames.

Gordon Matta-Clark
Splitting
1974
Gelatin silver print
40.6 x 50.8
San Fransisco Museum of Modern Art

2

Still, a distinction must be made between the cuts executed by Gordon Matta-Clark through various buildings and a crack. A crack is not 'designed' and as such, in principle, has no 'author'. Its path through built structure responds to the field of forces surrounding it. A cut could be finite, a stable state whereas a crack is a stage in a subsequent potential process of destruction. Cracks, of course, could also settle and close if the intensity of the contradictions within the force field surrounding them subsides.

3

Sous les pavés, la plage! – 'Beneath the paving stones, the beach!' was an anonymous graffiti, inspired by the Situationists, found in Paris in 1968.

the history of racism, running parallel to the history of modernity and … its untold dark side.'

Salcedo's assault on the architecture of Tate Modern may bring to mind two obvious landmark works of the last century: The 'building cuts' – with which, from 1971 until his death in 1978 – Gordon Matta-Clark 'un-walled' domestic and industrial interiors;[2] and *Germania* – the 'sledgehammer denunciations' of Hans Haacke, with which he pulverised the stone-tiled floor of the Nazi-era German pavilion at the 1993 Venice Biennale. These works demonstrated the power of art to operate 'against architecture' – against the very architecture that hosts it. As a form of architectural 'institutional critique', they sought to examine the conditioning of their own activity in relation to the ideological and economic frames of the gallery, with the ultimate goal of breaking out of what Georges Bataille called 'the architectural straitjacket' in search of liberation from the 'oppressive order of architecture'. Salcedo's crack in the floor of Tate does not offer any such hope of liberation. Under the pavement of the Turbine Hall nothing like the Situationists' beach is to be found;[3] the crack does not offer an escape from the discontent of urban culture but seeks to expose the terror of the past and bring it up to haunt the surface of our present.

Indeed, the building's various pasts coincide with a certain archaeology of post-war British history. The Bankside Power

Seismic crack
Loma Prieta, California, Earthquake October 17, 1989. Summit Road area in the Santa Cruz Mountains. A crack system destroyed a driveway adjacent to Summit Road half a mile southeast of Highway 17.

Aerial view of Bankside Power Station, Southwark
March 1963

Station,where Tate Modern is now located, was commissioned in 1947 to help power the needs of the reconstruction and growth of post-war London.[4] This was the time when the beginning of the British decolonisation process (in India, Pakistan, Palestine and Israel) led to extensive labour-migration flows (from East Asia, Africa and the Caribbean). The colonial geographies and economies of a decommissioning Empire were thereafter folded into the ethnic and spatial differences of inner cities. The new multicultural, multiracial metropolis inaugurated new forms of social exclusion and racial conflict. These took place in the new interstitial spaces – the housing estates, schools, workplace and hospitals – of a recently established welfare state that seemed otherwise grounded in the fantasy of social fusion and unity. If the building was constructed to coincide with the inauguration of the British welfare state, its use as a power station ended in 1982, with the Thatcher-government dismantling what was left of it. The cleansed and renovated modern ruin reopened in 2000 as Tate Modern, barely a year before the fatal acceleration of the 'War on Terror' reawakened the ghosts of a colonial past.

This return of dormant colonial practices is what critical geographer Derek Gregory has called the 'colonial present'[5] – a world that is looking forward but moving backwards, culturally (seemingly) post-colonial but politically regressing into a new form of colonialism. In fighting the dangers they helped produce, its new security forces and apparatuses have grown to saturate global geographies and the entirety of social life,

4
It was designed in 'gothic-modernist' style by the architect Giles Gilbert Scott, also known for his designs for Battersea Power station and the post office K2 phone booth, the source of the red British phone booth, a structure that similarly refused the simple utilitarian forms of modernism for a quaint, iconic vernacularism loved by so many.

5
Derek Gregory, The Colonial Present, Oxford 2004.

6
Olivier Razac, Barbed Wire: A Political History,
New York 2000; see also Reviel Netz, Barbed
Wire: An Ecology of Modernity, *Middletown 2004.*

while in the name of internal political order, programmes such as 'homeland security' equate safety with ordered domesticity. This colonial present is simultaneously marked by increased de-territorialisation and trans-border connectivity for the global rich and increased territorialised segregation and exclusion for the global poor. Its political surfaces themselves started splintering into a territorial patchwork of discontinuous fragments, set apart and fortified by makeshift barriers, temporary boundaries or invisible security apparatuses, and selectively woven together by transnational military, political or financial networks. The complex compartmentalised systems of these split geographies produced the notion that some people were 'irredeemably' different, thus licensing the unleashing of 'redeeming' violence upon them. Instead of the illusionary promise of a smooth and networked 'flat world', we have found ourselves negotiating the fragments of a fenced-up apartheid planet.

The wire fence embedded within the inner cuts of the crack indexes the instrument most associated with these colonial practices of separation, thus marking their return. The history of wire fencing, much like that of barbed wire, is grounded in that of nineteenth-century colonialism. A simple invention (or rather inversion) – the use of industrial-revolution-era developments in mechanical cloth-weaving techniques into weaving with steel wires – allowed these new types of fencings to be mass-produced and sold cheaply on a roll. They thus became the most common, almost ubiquitous, form of barriers to movement and of the making of enclosures. They were of particular use in the 'new worlds', whose frontiers were then pushed from shore-lines ever deeper inland. The territorial pattern of frontier expansion was irregular; it shifted with changing climate and geology. Pouring across pastoral grasslands with grids and parallels of fences and roads, it followed the narrow and splintering arteries of geological strata, tracing subterranean ridges of metal and mineral concentrations, or occupied fenced-up 'islands' above isolated fields of energy resources. Lines of engagement, marked by these makeshift boundaries, were not limited to the edges of political space but existed throughout its depth.

In *Barbed Wire: A Political History*[6] Oliver Razac claimed that it was the technology of mass-producing these simple means of enclosure that opened up, in the second half of the nineteenth century, a condition of systematic and ever-present enclosure and fortification. Because machine-woven wire fencing was cheap, light, fast to erect and dismantle, it made territorial-separation ever more ubiquitous, privatising the possibility of relatively effective enclosures. Fences allowed space to be parcelled out and commodified, and protected it from the very people from whom it was taken. The constantly shifting borders of private farms shrunk the space for native populations, who were themselves referred to as 'predators', no different from those in the natural environment. The multiplicity of various fences marked a growing archipelago of exclusion that was more than a simple territorial delimitation; it was a cultural/political separation between two polarised spaces: a protective, domesticated inside and a wild, threatening outside. This mutual extraterritoriality also marked the difference between two distinct kinds of lives – one precious and valuable, and the other worthless and expandable. The borders of space thus became the margins of life. The open weave made the fences suitable for optical surveillance (since one could see through them) and control (since one could shoot through them).[7] They were chosen, like other apparatuses of control, according to the simple logic of expending the smallest amount of energy and resources for the maximum effects of control. By designating and constraining habitats, by physically marking out the limit of different types of spaces, they have become administrative devices for the creation and maintenance of a demographic separation and for population control.[8] Ever-multiplying 'border devices' characterised the territorial physiognomy of separation and the performative force of colonial administration.

In a return to these spatial physiognomies of the colonial era, contemporary political space has now grown to resemble a territorial patchwork of introverted enclaves – a growing archipelago of externally alienated and internally homogeneous enclaves outside the control of the territories surrounding them. Various other zones – zones of political piracy, zones of crisis, zones of barbaric violence, zones of 'humanitarian catastrophes', zones of full citizenship, no citizenship or 'weak citizenship' are located side by side, each within the other, simultaneously and in unprecedented proximities. The dynamic

7
By this logic it must be said that the concrete wall built through Palestinian cities is a regression from the principle that affirms the power of vision. Throughout most of its length, however, when running through rural rather than urban areas, it is made of barbed-wire fencing.

8
The first time that fences and barbed wire were used explicitly to control populations was during the Boer War (1899–1902) fought to protect South Africa's newly discovered gold mines, when British forces imprisoned Afrikaans in the world's first concentration camps.

Boer War Camp c.1900
A camp for British prisoners of war at Waterval during the Boer War. The huts are made of corrugated iron.

morphology of contemporary frontier-territories is an evolving image of transformation; borders ebb and flow, creep along, stealthily surrounding buildings, roads, transport hubs, villages and cities. The scar tissue of the splintering multitude of contemporary digital or physical 'separations' is a series of cracks cutting across multiple sites: local or regional fortifications, embassies, residential enclaves, military camps, off-shore production zones, mineral extraction sites, airports, as well as the shadow zones of the dispossessed: ad-hoc detention centres, occupied by refugees, 'illegal' immigrants, asylum seekers and other undesirable 'suspects'.

Ruins over ruins: under the destroyed floor of the Turbine Hall, the inner faces of the crack reveal the material ruins of empire and colonisation; these in turn lend themselves to various critical readings of counter-archaeology that threaten to destroy the shield of its history. But what lies open is merely one of several potential spasmodic eruptions (along yet unseen fault lines) of violent pasts onto the condensed surface of the present. In a time past, the teleology of progress, all historical moments could share a single plain with multiple possible cracks – lines of destruction – to connect between them. Tate Modern is already itself a ruin, one of the many cleansed ruins of industrial modernity turned public institution. The crack in its floor signals the beginning of a further process of ruination – the ruination of the already ruined. The crack now running through its floor might be just one stage in a process of unfolding sequences of destruction beyond control.

Earth Aches: the Aesthetics of the Cut
Mieke Bal

In an exhibition space so monumental as to require works especially made for it, one expects something huge. The Turbine Hall of Tate Modern is so enormous that one needs the spatial reassurance of an artwork that fills it. Scale, in other words, is the common denominator for the annual commissions. For this space, Doris Salcedo has proposed something less than huge. Instead, ignoring the height of the hall, she has made an inscription on the floor. This word is to be taken literally: 'in-', as in insertion, invasion, incorporation, and 'scription', as in writing. For her acts of engraving, she uses a cutting instrument that leaves indelible traces. The result of her intervention is a negative space, an emptiness not remedied but exacerbated; a space cut into two halves that are each other's negatives.

Yet, this negativity is as ambitious as the hall is enormous. No object is placed in the space, yet 'the work', the inscription, the negative sculpture traverses it in its entirety. It is not just a sign or representation of something. It signifies nothing, and at the same time, because of that negativity, everything. For, the negative, logically, is encompassing; it harbours everything that is not stipulated in its positive counterpart. Hence, in the empty hall, the inscripted negative space opens up an abyss of unlimited meaning. Here, absence is the trace, the physical memory of violence, like an enormous scar. If the scale of the Turbine Hall can be seen as an experiential and semiotic totality, then the inscription encompasses it all.

First, the ground on which the inscription has been applied is in pain; and that ground is 'all' – the earth. Second, the cut divides. The hall, the earth, is cut into two halves, and between these, nothing. Nothing includes everything that has disappeared into the abyss, like history, seen as wilful amnesia and its aftermath; the history of the present in which history vanishes, leaves its scars only for those who care to see it, helped by the artist, who insists on showing the scar. Interpreted in

reminiscent terms of the art of the twentieth century – cinema – we could see what Salcedo has done here as an *aesthetics of the cut*.

The cut of montage is the negative space where the imagination is activated. One needs to fill in the gaps. From one sequence to the next, 'nothing' asks to be turned into narrative. Salcedo's work is not narrative, however. It has been consistent in its passionately meticulous preoccupation with politics, memory and the pain of others. But this artist tells no stories. For over two decades, she has been working over extant material things to make them sites of grief. While the things stubbornly hold on to whatever they were before, she takes them on, she rubs, scrapes, paints and otherwise adds to them, to abduct them from the realm of household invisibility and turn them into memorials of loss.

Looking at the world obliquely, from the a-central position of the artist engaged with it, Salcedo handles materials as a form of 'hopeless mourning'. By vocation displaced, according to her definition of the artist, she rubs the past into the present object and in so doing she blocks the process of forgetting. Art can do that; it can enforce a gaze that, in spite of the fragility of 'a passing caress', will itself bear the traces of the horror encrusted in the work. Horror, not the narratives of it: this is the key affect that Salcedo inscribes without sentimentality.[1]

With a consistency bordering on obsession, Salcedo nevertheless experiments tirelessly with a great variety of aesthetic strategies, as if never entirely convinced that the affective power she has conjured up through one of these could suffice. She seeks to make art that does not belong to her; she is not interested in leaving her signature, but instead considers art a means to affect the world outside of herself. Art able to produce a knowledge greater than that of the person making it; a knowledge not reducible to individual psychology, nor to the great categories of sociology; a knowledge constantly in movement, because its fragile articulations can only occur in relationship to viewers, users, or readers of it. It is also the product of collaboration and dialogue. This does not mean the obvious collaboration with co-workers, but the social buzzing around her to which she responds.

And each new strategy, it turns out, although not necessarily foregrounded, was already present in the previous one. I will briefly outline her aesthetic strategies as I see them, without assigning these to 'periods' of her production. In fact, they often coincide, reinforcing one another. They are treated separately here, only to demonstrate the complexity of the aesthetics of an art that seeks to intervene in the world; an art that seeks to be political because it is aesthetic, and vice versa. There is no tension between art and politics here; art can only be art if it is political.

La Casa Viuda IV (detail)
1994
Wood, fabric and bones
257.5 x 46.5 x 33
Private Collection, London

1
All views I attribute here to the artist have been drawn from the interview with Carlos Basualdo in Nancy Princenthal, Carlos Basualdo, Andreas Huyssen (eds), Doris Salcedo, *London 2000.*

The first strategy is the insertion of barely visible *anthropomorphisms*. In many of her sculptures, such as the *Casa Viuda* series (1992–4), some human form – or a trace of it – insists that the past of the objects must not be erased. A small anthropomorphic presence – a child's dress, a piece of torn fabric, a zipper in the wood of a desk, bones, or kitchen utensils – remains in a surface otherwise elaborated like a great abstract painting. Thus, the artist has inserted herself into modernism only to subvert it from within, acknowledging its power, yet declaring it inadequate to the mission of political art. Whether or not these small but insistent anthropomorphic traces were metaphorical or materially real, the metonymic principle at work safeguarded the presence of the victims of violence, otherwise disappeared. This oblique, near-invisible presence of the human form recalls the predominance of the representation of the human body in the history of Western art. It recalls art's complicity: in its acts of honouring the human body that inevitably erased those bodies that violence had dishonoured. Beauty and pain are bound together. Meanwhile, one of Salcedo's most widely known and exhibited works, *Atrabiliarios*, from 1991–3, pursued the question of the human form to the extreme, and beyond. Rather than being small presences, here, the traces of people are all there is. The worn shoes embedded in niches in gallery walls are among the most gripping traces of human presence. They have been worn and worn out, have taken the shape of the individual foot, and supported those walking the earth in search of a life. Thus, they are powerful metaphors, the more potent because they are metonymic, showing the real, negative form of the foot.

The paradigmatic status of the footprint in semiotic theory over-determines the effect of the shoe as an index of presence past. The history of violence of the twentieth century further over-determines the power of worn shoes. After mass violence – indeed, after genocide – what remains are heaps of shoes, mountains of them, testifying to the lives lost. For each two shoes, one person died. Shoes, especially in large quantities, carry what has been called a 'holocaust effect'.[2]

But Salcedo did not heap the shoes into piles. Instead, she individualised them, burying each one in the negative space of the niches in the wall, and then covering it with animal skin. Thus, through a second strategy, of *translation*, she retrieved the singular from the abstraction of generality. At the same time, the translucent animal skin that covers the niches – itself over-determined as an artistic conveyer of a Holocaust effect – decreases the readability of the shoes. She thus reworked metaphor and its discontents, confronting this rhetorical figure with the need for translation (literally the Latinate synonym of the Greek word 'metaphor'), so that singularity can be preserved, precariously, and yet brought to affective performance in other places. Only

Atrabiliarios
1992–2004
Shoes, animal fibre and surgical thread
Dimensions variable
San Francisco Museum of Modern Art

Overleaf:
Atrabiliarios (detail)
1991–93
Shoes, animal fibre and surgical thread
Dimensions variable
Pulitzer Foundation, St. Louis

2
The term 'holocaust effect' stems from a very relevant study of aesthetic strategies in facing mass violence: Ernst van Alphen, Caught by History: Holocaust Effects in Art, Literature, and Theory, *Stanford, CA 1997.*

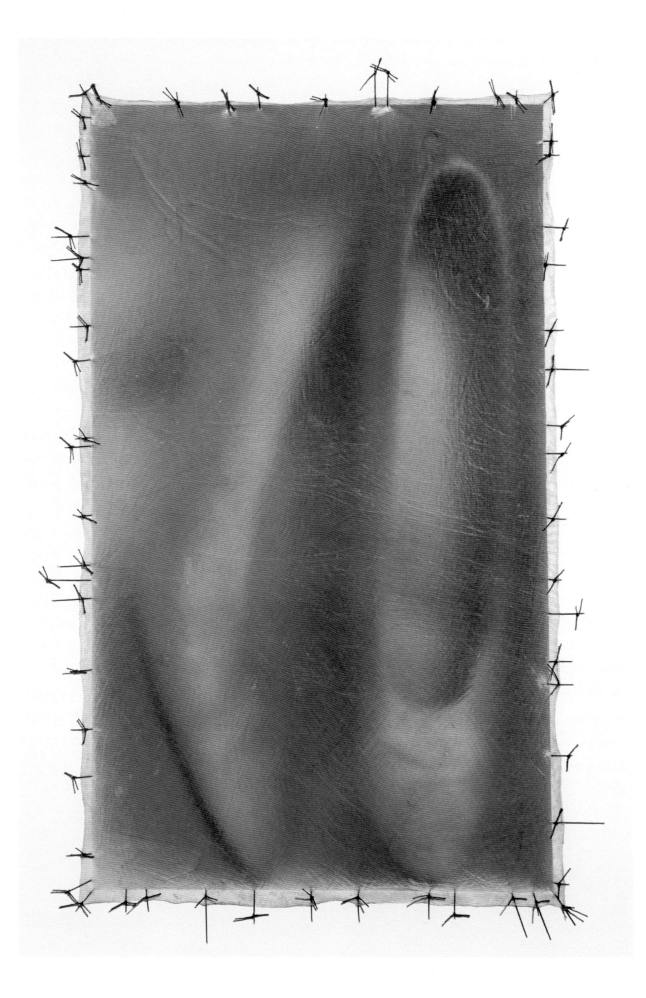

3
I have developed this in 'Metaphoring: Making a Niche of Negative Space', Maria Margaroni, Effie Yiannopoulou (eds), Metaphoricity and the Politics of Mobility, *Amsterdam and New York 2006 pp.159–80. The term 'holding environment' comes from object-relations theory in psychoanalysis. It has been brought to bear on contemporary art by Janneke Lam,* Whose Pain? Childhood, Trauma, Imagination, *Amsterdam 2002.*

through such work that places singularity in a 'holding environment' while making its affect accessible elsewhere, can art be effectively political.[3]

In other sculptures, such as the *Unland* series (1997), the focus of the aesthetics, but not of the politics, shifted. There, Salcedo deploys a third strategy: working with *duration*. These works performed temporal solicitations of their viewers, demanding them to donate considerable time to victims from whom we tend to look away because their pain disturbs. These are the works where, on the one hand, the fragility of the surfaces is daunting, so that one barely dares to approach; on the other hand, they are hardly visible as art, and one feels beckoned to take a closer look. The point is that looking at the sculptures requires surrender; not to a shape of grief, but to its temporality.

There are three distorted tables in the *Unland* series, each constructed out of two tables whose legs have been sawn off and whose tops are slightly discrepant, looking a sickly grey in some places. At the distance from which I first saw them, they didn't look like artworks at all. I thought I had walked into a near-empty warehouse. Alternatively, from close up, the forms become invisible and one sees only a painterly *surface.* Here, one mobilises one's anthropomorphic imagination and sees something resembling the skin of scar tissue. The surface consists of hundreds of tiny follicles, crisscrossing threads of tattered, translucent silk, and on one table is a child's cot, sunk into the wooden planks of the table's surface and sewn onto it, by means of human hair. In order to see that, though, viewers had to peer, bend over, go near then recede in horror, and approach again to ascertain that what they saw was 'really' that material trace of human life. This requires duration: the donation of time, made inevitable by means of what I term *temporal foreshortening*.

The aesthetic strategies of anthropomorphism, translation and temporal foreshortening, all uniquely Salcedo's inflections of political art, are especially powerful due to a fourth strategy, which brings us closer to *Shibboleth*. This is, to put it simply, *installation*. In her version of it, installation is not about the harmony of display. On the contrary, she seeks to achieve disharmony, misfits. Through the breaks between work and surroundings, she foregrounds an out-of-placeness for the work. Just as she seeks to bracket her personal signature in favour of what she has called an 'active anonymity', she also brackets the autonomy of the artwork, another of those tenacious dogmas of modernism, and puts it in tension with these dogmas. This autonomy is always illusory, yet desired, a desire not surprising in an art world that remains organised around name and fame.

Salcedo's works are always installed with extreme care, so that space and light engage in critical dialogue. Lighting is thus an integral part of

4
*On the productivity of acknowledged complicity,
see Gayatri Chakravorty Spivak,* A Critique of
Post-colonial Reason: Toward a History of the
Vanishing Present, *Cambridge 1999.*

(Top)
Unland
Installation view at SITE Santa Fe, 1998

Foreground
Unland
the orphan's tunic
1997
Wood, cloth, hair
80 x 245 x 98
Caixa Forum, Barcelona

Background left
Unland
audible in the mouth
1998
Wood, thread, hair
74.5 x 315 x 80
Tate

Background right
Unland
irreversible witness
1995–98
Wood, cloth, metal, hair
112 x 249 x 89
San Francisco Museum of Modern Art

(Bottom left)
Unland
the orphan's tunic
1997
Wood, cloth, hair
80 x 245 x 98
Caixa Forum, Barcelona

(Bottom right)
Unland
audible in the mouth
1998
Wood, thread, hair
74.5 x 315 x 80
Tate

the sculpture, and so is the space around it. Sometimes, the works are placed at odd angles to the viewer, suggesting a warehouse rather than an exhibition. The difficult visual access intimates modesty, the need to be discreet, the sense of intrusion into other people's lives; hence, our inevitable complicity, which can be productive only if it is recognised. Sometimes, in contrast, an even, gloomy light reinforces the sense of loss the pieces embody, as well as the incapacity to absorb the conditions of that loss. [4]

From these installations one may already surmise that *site-specificity* is going to be another, fifth aesthetic strategy. *Abyss*, the work built in Castello de Rivoli in 2006, is key in this sense. The site, an eighteenth-century space within the castle of Rivoli, a space once used by Carlo Emanuele III to immure his father King Vittorio Amedeo, was already quite like what the artist then proceeded to make of it. It had a huge brick vaulted dome. Working, 'simply', to lower this vault by extending its walls downwards, Salcedo built the perimeter so as to lower the sides and construct a more literal, less invisible prison. Extending the walls so low that the windows opening to the outside only remained visible as a tantalising but inaccessible world of light and freedom, she made the wall literally weigh down. She thus created a space that was at the same time empty and enclosed. This theme of enclosure is another example of the rich complexity of Salcedo's work. It was already immanent in, for example, the grey, confining light in the installation of *Tenebrae (Noviembre 6, 1985)*, exhibited 1999–2000 in the Camden Arts Centre in London, but in Rivoli it is taken to its literal extremity.

The vault or abyss weighs down not only on the visitor but also on time itself, which is suspended in an in-between moment. How does the imprisonment of a king by his own son 'translate' into contemporary politics? How does the particularity of this historical event become of such contemporary urgency that it needs to be put upon us with such monumental gravity? This is an instance of that act of translation from the singular to a qualified accessibility; that act through which we can and must be in touch with the suffering of others. The violence, this time, is qualified as imprisoning, suffocating immurement. The 'site-specifity' resides in that momentary experience of being held prisoner by one's own. Instead of a king's castle, the work invokes by antiphrasis the detention centres where people are held, sometimes to deadly peril. The assault on the freedom of those who suffer confinement in the contemporary world is brought home with great, indeed monumental, power.

This last phrase brings in a sixth aesthetic strategy that underlies every artistic gesture Salcedo has ever made. This is the entangled and polemical relationship of her sculpture to *monumentality*. Monuments relate to memory and to scale, and Salcedo addresses both these

Tenebrae (Noviembre 6, 1985)
1999–2000
Lead and steel
193 x 561.5 x 555
Private Collection, Vancouver

Previous:
Abyss
Installation view, Triennial of Contemporary
Art, Castello di Rivoli, Turin
2005
Brick, cement, steel and epoxy resin
441 x 1386 x 1624

Noviembre 6 y 7
Palace of Justice, Bogotá
2002

5
This can be considered an instance of a 'preposterous history' within the work of a single artist. See my book Quoting Caravaggio: Contemporary Art, Preposterous History, *Chicago 1999 for this concept, which, I suggest, Salcedo also brings to bear on the histories she re-activates in her work. On the French monuments, see Pierre Nora's term lieu de mémoire in 'Between Memory and History: Les Lieux de Memoire',* Representations 26, Spring 1989, pp.7–24. For the German monuments, see Andreas Huyssen , 'Monumental Seduction', Mieke Bal, Jonathan Crewe and Leo Spitzer (eds),* Acts of Memory: Cultural Recall in the Present, *Hanover 1999, pp.191–207.*

6
The term 'affection image' refers to Gilles Deleuze's tripartite categorisation of images – perception image, affection image, and action image. See Cinema 1: the Movement-Image, *trans. Hugh Tomlinson and Barbara Habberjam, Minneapolis, 1986, pp.66–70. On the possibility that objects can actually transmit affect, see Ernst van Alphen, 'Affective Operations in Art and Literature' (forthcoming).*

aspects over and again. In general – and this would be extremely relevant for an artist like Salcedo – monuments are tokens of memory. In France, for example, everywhere, down to the smallest villages, there is a 'Monument aux Morts', mostly a conventional memorial to the unknown soldiers who died for the glory of the fatherland. One wonders if their omnipresence, as well as their traditional aesthetics, render such monuments invisible, and the aptly named 'unknown' soldiers even more dead and forgotten.

Recently, attempts to build monuments to commemorate mass violence such as the Holocaust have focused on invisibility, such as a buried library or a list of names slowly sinking into the ground. The latter seeks to incorporate the temporal dimension of history into its spatial strategy. None of these attempts matches the powerful gesture of retrieving removed histories, in order to enrich the surface of the present, to which Salcedo's *Abyss* testified. Retrospectively, all those painterly surfaces of her earlier works receive an intensifying gloss.[5]

The height where the brick walls of *Abyss* leave off is about 120 cm. For most adult viewers, this is lower than eye level, leaving a space shorter than body height, so that the outside remains alluring but strictly invisible. The wall is visually suspended, so that one feels the suspense of time. A temporal breath-stopping suspension: will the wall continue to descend and immure us completely? Salcedo's answer to monumentality, then, is to bring in time by suspending it; the suspension of time that counters time's erasures into eternity. The wall has been a theme in other works as well. In *Noviembre 6 y 7*, a performance from 2002, innumerable chairs slowly descended along the wall of the new Palace of Justice in Bogotá, a non-descript structure built after the massacre of over a hundred civilians including most of the Palace's judges, when thirty-five guerrillas had invaded the palace. The descent of Salcedo's chairs lasted for the duration of the violent event, which the artist had witnessed all those years ago. The chairs, empty of their occupants, became the wall, the facade behind which the dark side of state power hid its terror; and thus the wall came down with them. In Istanbul, a four-storey space of 142 square metres was completely filled with chairs that became constitutive of the space behind the walls where displaced people had become invisible, in the relentless temporal linearity of globalisation. Mobility, under conditions of displacement, equals a form of incarceration.

These works redefine monumentality. Refusing to relinquish that mode of turning public space into an 'affection image'[6] that holds the viewer and slows down the time conducive to forgetting, Salcedo instead recaptures the memorising function of monumentality. Thus, she reconstitutes monuments as social

Installation, 8th International Istanbul Biennial
2003

7
Martin Heidegger, The Question of Technology
and Other Essays, *trans. William Lovitt,*
New York 1977, p.135.

spaces where intimacy and politics meet; where the ruptured intimacy of others, affectively experienced, cries out for political action. Sculpture is the art form par excellence that addresses the shared responsibility of and for space. This is why, I speculate, this artist who works surfaces as if competing with the most successful abstract painters, stays well away from abstraction in her sculptures – as far, that is, as she stays away from representation. This is why, moreover, those works that are human in scale – the scale of the people whom she seeks to keep alive in our memories – are installed in large spaces such as the cathedral in Liverpool, the empty second floor of the New Museum in New York, the large empty spaces with shiny floors and gloomy light in the Camden Arts Centre. Or the exterior wall of a state building.

In addition to memory, monumentality is always, also, an issue of scale. *Scale*, the shock of disproportion, is yet another of Salcedo's aesthetic strategies to make political art. In this she joins a 'baroque' critical inquiry into visibility and harmony, denaturalising as well as validating human scale as the measure of all things. Martin Heidegger sees in the deployment of gigantism a historical phenomenon. In his famous essay 'The Age of the World Picture', he hints at the paradoxical nature of this phenomenon:

> Everywhere and in the most varied forms and disguises the gigantic is making its appearance. In so doing, it evidences itself simultaneously in the tendency toward the increasingly small … The gigantic presses forward in a form that actually seems to make it disappear – in the annihilation of great distances by the airplane, in the setting before us of foreign and remote worlds in their everydayness, which is produced at random through radio by a flick of the hand.[7]

The works by Salcedo that employ scale – and many of them do – denaturalise the 'everydayness' of this wavering between the exceedingly huge and the infinitely small by means of the insertion of human scale. Hence, when she was invited to make a work for the huge Turbine Hall, it was inevitable that she would deploy that seventh strategy: scale. This strategy affects all the aesthetic modes outlined so far.

The small, anthropomorphic lower part of *La Casa Viuda I* (1992–4), or the zipper discreetly incrusted in *La Casa Viuda II* (1993–4) are effective exactly because, while human in dimensions, they are integrated in a form that exceeds their size by far. The shoes in *Atrabiliarios* are shocking precisely because of their very real size. The temporal foreshortening that I consider the aesthetic operational mode of *Unland* unleashes an effect of scale that, as in *Atrabiliarios*, works through the sense that reality itself is out of proportion. The

La Casa Viuda II
1993–94
Wood, fabric, metal and bone
259.70 x 79.7 x 60.3

child's cot is real size, but seems pathetically small simply because of the emptiness that surrounds it, which was, in that case, the site-specificity of the work as installed. The human hairs used to sew are so thin it is hard to see them, even once seen. This makes time circular, and our engagement with the work durational. And of course, in *Abyss*, the emptiness surrounding many of the earlier works is the very matter of the work.

In Tate Modern, Salcedo contends with a space that recalls another aspect of *Abyss*, an eighth aesthetic strategy that the artist never leaves out of sight in her elaborate work on surface. This is *labour* – the inhumane exploitation that keeps sections of humanity so near slavery. Building that vault against gravity to make gravity – in Rivoli, capitalistically absurd – was an act of solidarity with the downtrodden of the earth, an attempt to experience in weeks and weeks of physically hard labour what many experience during their entire lives. Labour as aesthetic strategy is an attempt to experience the suffering of others, to demonstrate the impossibility of remaining outside what one critiques, and yet, at the same time, when deploying it in something so 'useless' as this empty artwork, attempting to defeat capitalism. The title refers to this: building an abyss, a gap, is yet another act of negativity. The crushing weight of the exercise of oppression fills the empty space. It fills it, totally, with the murmurings of innumerable people whom power silences and erases.

With this in mind, enter the Turbine Hall. The space emphatically belongs to modernism – both in its previous function as a power station and in its current incarnation as a space where art can boast its importance, its monumental proportions. Salcedo plays with this monumentality, takes it at its word, so to speak. She leaves it entirely empty, and fills it with the entire world: its divisions, its histories, its differences, its repressions – the scar tissue of all of the above. The title refers to a Biblical linguistic test of authenticity, of belonging to the privileged. This reference indicates that divisions are always already hierarchical. The Ephraimites, who could not pronounce the 'sh' in the word 'shibboleth' were classified immediately by the Gileadites as dangerous, as enemies, and killed. Whether this phonetic test is applied to ancient or contemporary Israel, or to the US, where at the Canadian border a friend of mine was asked to pronounce 'Toronto', or figuratively, to all tests of belonging, from resident permits to passports, does not matter. Like all signs, especially linguistic ones, the 's' versus 'sh' pronunciation of the word shibboleth is the arbitrary sign of either belonging to the side of privilege or being cast away as disposable, infra-humanity, subject to terror, and subsequently erased.

The negative space, a huge version of that of *Abyss*, remains open. One can enter and exit the hall at will. But once within visual reach

In this respect, the work invokes an entire field, so to speak, concerning borders. See Inge E. Boer, Uncertain Territories: Boundaries in Cultural Analysis, Amsterdam 2006.

of the work, the earth tears open as if during an earthquake. There is no comfort, no consolation for the destruction of the ground on which we stand. Again, the aesthetics of negativity traverse all the strategies previously deployed, to give them a new urgency. This time, no escape into particularity is even remotely possible. The viewer is addressed directly, relentlessly and violently. History is brought into the present with renewed force.

Everything here is concrete and literal. And yet, no facile reading can be made; no absorption of meaning will let the viewer escape into intellectual understanding. The negative space is literally bottomless. Just as the chasm produced by a serious earthquake cannot be really looked into, gazing into the jagged line that traverses the hall will yield no images. And because we cannot see the bottom, there is none; epistemology equals ontology. Sculptors traditionally carve into stone until beautiful form emerges and Pygmalion shows his power. Here, the carving goes downwards into the depth of the concrete floor, and no beauty is unearthed. Beauty is disqualified, no longer allowed to define what it is to be European. For, as this piece indicts, beauty is complicit with domination and exclusion, with the division that this piece embodies and, in doing so, paradoxically brings to light. There is no beauty here.

And yet, once visitors get closer, once they dare peer into the crevice, they find a negative sculpture. Cast concrete with metal fencing deeply encrusted into it resists the very idea of emptiness. The crevice has walls, and these have surfaces on the level of loving elaboration so typical for the artist. In other artworks surface may be nothing but superficial beauty. In Salcedo's work, it is the unexpected site of homage, labour and care. No one will disappear. The crevice opens up the world's primary division as a field inside which things go on; where people live. The border is not a line but a space, negative or rather, made negative, but not really empty. Here, in the surfaces of that deep crevice's walls, lies Salcedo's humble aesthetic; her angry optimism.[8]

Her art lies deeply buried. Art has collaborated with the moral and aesthetic canons that elevated one part of humanity over the others. As opposed to lack of historical reflection on domination, our universities and museums maintain, that art does have a history – 'the history of art', evolving in ever-increasing sophistication, away from the imagined primitive beginnings. And because of the ideology of origin underlying standard Western thought, archaeology in particular is, as the French language has it, *traduit en justice* – brought to court, or literally, 'translated into justice'. Hence, the carving into the immeasurable depth of the earth. From the womb of the earth in the not-so-distant past, the justification for European domination was exhumed, in Asia, in Africa, in the name of European classicism. Attempts to change that history met and still meet with violent opposition.[9]

Such defensive opposition is symptomatic of the enormous stakes; as enormous as the Turbine Hall and its floor. 'Enormous', then, is the hub around which the meanings and effects of this work circle. This measure of scale is brought to bear on Salcedo's ninth aesthetic strategy: *language*. For it is in conceptions of language that her practice of what I have called above 'translation' is best understood. Cutting through – to literalise another phrase – the ground we stand on in the Turbine Hall, she also cuts through any attempt to hide behind metaphor, figurativeness, symbolism. The title *Shibboleth* stands for a loyalty to language and a disabused awareness of its inevitable performativity of separation. The cut here is, first of all, to be taken literally. As much as it may hurt.[10]

The scar that this gargantuan work constitutes, is, in the first place, a literal one: the trace of a deep pain, a cut that has divided the entire world. And lest we attempt to hide behind history, Salcedo brings this pain into the present. She has destroyed the floor, the ground, on this gigantic scale, as a tiny portion of a cut that really runs through the entire globe. It pervades everyone's life, private and public; it runs between and within cities, countries and continents. Institutional racism is so pervasive that we even fail to notice it; we now call it 'multiculturalism' or 'post-coloniality', and all, it seems, is well. Not so, says this piece. And rubbing it in by means of scale, Salcedo simultaneously uses art, that smallest of contributions, to finesse the message.

The painstaking work, the labour on the surfaces of the two sides of the crevice, performs that finessing. This labour pays homage to the people left on the other side of the divide, and hence, in the abyss of underprivileged life. It insists that borders are spaces, in all their negativity. Even this labour is subject to the disproportional scale. No monumental proportion will allow the work to take shortcuts, if only because the people brought to memory are not cut any slack either. Every square inch of this enormous double surface has been delicately worked, carved, cast and mended, its fencing, heavy with meaning, encrusted in its sides. Inside the crevice that divides the world, another fencing system commemorates the internal cages in which people have been, and still are, confined like animals.

The means of art, the one where freedom and slow time are still possible – specifically, the means of sculpture, that art of social space – allow the production of that disconcerting pain that forces us to stop and foreshorten duration. As with Salcedo's earlier work, this cut requires slow processing, or else there is nothing to see but

9
A central case for the prosecution is the controversy around Martin Bernal's daring, two-volume study, vehemently contradicted. Martin Bernal, Black Athena: The AfroAsiatic Roots of Classical Civilization, *Brunswick, NJ 1987; Jacques Berlinerblau,* Heresy in the University: The Black Athena Controversy and the Responsibilities of American Intellectuals. *Brunswick, NJ 1999; Martin Bernal,* Black Athena Writes Back: Martin Bernall Responds to his Critics, *Durham, NC 2001.*

10
On language's power to hurt, see Judith Butler, Excitable Speech: A Politics of the Performative, *New York 1997.*

11
*On the gaze as the world looking back,
see the works of Kaja Silverman,
especially her* World Spectators.

damage. The hall remains empty, but the cut through its concrete floor is, ultimately, also anthropomorphic. For it is in the flesh of human beings, that huge underclass of world citizens excluded from the minimal conditions of humanity, that cuts such as these have been and continue to be made. At the edge of social life, the people affected by the great divide are, for once, central to art.

At odds, violently so, with the rational parameters of the building the jagged scar gapes at us. As Jacques Lacan and others have argued, the object looks back; our gaze is embedded in the gaze of others. Against the fierce, constant labour to keep the holders of that accusatory gaze at bay, casting them into invisibility and forgetfulness, this cut, from the depths of the carver's knife, does look back. For, as cinema has taught us, it is in the empty, negative space of the cut that the viewer's imagination is set to work. The aesthetics of the cut encompasses all the other aesthetics that this indispensable artist has explored. With an impressive optimism, Salcedo allows us to see the unseeable, in order for the scar of the earth to heal.[11]

Proposal for a project for the Turbine Hall, Tate Modern, London, 2007

'The absolute orientation of the Same towards the Other could be captured in a Greek term – liturgy – that in its first signification means the exercise of an office that is not only totally gratuitous, but requires from the executants an investment at a loss. This uncompensated work, this liturgy, is not sited as a cult alongside "works" and ethics. It is ethics itself.'
Emanuel Levinas

Shibboleth, the piece I propose to inscribe in the Turbine Hall, is an attempt to orient this modernist space towards the unbridgeable gap that separates humanity from infra-humanity.

Shibboleth is a negative space: it addresses the w(hole) in history that marks the bottomless difference that separates whites from non-whites. The w(hole) in history that I am referring to is the history of racism, which runs parallel to the history of modernity, and is its untold dark side.

Modernity is seen as an exclusively European event, in which the self-cultivation of the human mind through the exercise of reason and the study of the classics had as its main purpose the creation of a homogeneous, rational and beautiful society. This has been the official version of the history of modernity. In this narration colonial and imperial history has been disregarded, marginalised or simply obliterated.

The forgetfulness of imperial enterprises has played an active role in shaping the image Europe has of itself. Paul Gilroy says that this image alleviates the ethical obligation owed by Europe to the rest of the planet, and it also allows the continuation of the privileges racial hierarchy has institutionalised.

In this image the presence of non Europeans, or, as they are now called, 'post-colonial peoples', is widely perceived as the sole vector of decadence, capable of jeopardising the historical and cultural heritage that gave shape to Europe's identity.

Shibboleth is an attempt to address the section of humankind that has been left out of the history of modernity, and kept at the margin of high Western culture. Although I am well aware that this is nothing new, I simply want to address this issue from the perspective of art, analysing the role art played in the formation of the stereotype of human beauty. Through classical art a standard of human beauty was created, but the truly catastrophic element was brought about by the fact that this idealisation of human beauty supposedly reflected a superior moral order. The writings of Winckelmann or Burckhardt played an important role in the solidification of this timeless and unchangeable stereotype, present even nowadays.

Western art developed an ideal of humanity so restrictedly defined that it excluded non-European peoples from the human genre. This stereotype was central in the development of racism as a system of thought.

We are told racism is a symptom of a contemporary malaise, but the philosopher Jacques Rancière affirms that it is the disease itself. In his words: 'The disease, in fact, of consensus itself, is the loss of any measure of otherness. The transmogrification of the Other to the frenzied point of pure racist rejection.'

The piece I am proposing for the Turbine Hall is about absolute indifference. No cultural ornament attenuates the desolation and destitution it is addressing. This piece is inopportune and – apparently – out of control; it intrudes on the space of the Turbine Hall. Its occurrence seems to be the product of an irrational event crossing through a rationalist building. Its appearance disturbs the Turbine Hall in the same way the appearance of immigrants disturbs the consensus and homogeneity of European societies. In high Western tradition the inopportune that interrupts development, progress, is the immigrant, the one who does not share the identity of the identical and has nothing in common with the community.

The time in which we live is defined by the rational brutality and ruthless indifference racial hierarchy has instituted. Contemporary racism uses different strategies from twentieth-century racism, but both are equally capable of generating a condition of social death. Social death is the legacy of racism, and it means removing a man from humankind; it is to deprive a man of his humanity, or, as Paul Celan put it, it is 'death-in-life'.

I am focusing on this boundary because I believe it charts the position from which an artist today may address the experience of the great majority of human beings: a huge, socially excluded underclass that lives on the edges, on the epicentre of catastrophe, on the borders of life. They dwell in conditions where life is reduced to pure naked experience. Their experience defines my work.

Doris Salcedo
December 2006

Proposal for a Project for the Palace of Justice, Bogotá, 2002

On 6 and 7 November 2002 I will make an *Act of Memory* to mark the tragic events that occurred at the Palace of Justice in Bogotá on 6 and 7 November 1985.

This work will address a difficult moment in the country's history, which it has tried to forget. It hopes to capture forgotten fragments of the past and to present them to an audience who will witness this act. It will be a means to confront us with an image that will prevent us from forgetting, allowing victims' families, as well as the survivors, to set aside their private memories in order to form a collective memory.

I will create an ephemeral work of art – a commemorative piece – but very different to the traditional monuments that are often nationalistic and grandiose. My intention is to focus on the Palace of Justice as the location for this *Act of Memory*, a place where collective and individual memories alike will be encouraged.

The piece will begin on 6 November at 11.35 am, the time when the first victim was assassinated. At that precise moment, a wooden chair, bare and worn, will slowly be lowered over the façade of the south wall of the Palace. This action will be repeated several times. Sometimes the chairs will descend alone and on other occasions they will come down as a group all joined up together. Each one of them will move at a different speed, until the empty chairs cover the wall of the Palace's north-eastern corner. Approximately 300 chairs will be used to create this image of loss and absence, the legacy of this violent act. Slowly shifting for 53 hours on the Palace of Justice's façade, these chairs will mark a space and a time to remember and reflect.

It is important to understand that many of the city's inhabitants are themselves the bearers of this memory. For that reason I intend to generate an image that will jolt the memory of passers-by, so that they can confront their own memory of this terrible event. The idea is to present an image that rejects triumphant nationalism in an attempt to get closer to the realities of physical loss and the feeling of emptiness left behind by conflict. It is a work that deals with the tension between remembering and forgetting, a situation with which the survivors and those affected struggle, year in, year out. The work I am proposing finds itself at the crossroads between the desire to remember and the impulse to forget.

The empty chairs are statements of absence allowing one to be aware of the fragility of those who were behind those walls 17 years ago. Exposed and suspended on the stone façade, the empty chair emphasises the vulnerability, not only of those who worked in the Palace of Justice, but of us all. This piece is vulnerable from within and unprotected on the exterior.

One could say that art is impotent when confronting absolute power. Yet, it is precisely in this impotency and uselessness that poetry resides. It is through art that one regains the humanity that has been desecrated. As the philosopher Giorgio Agamben once explained: 'When the individual is conscious of his own demise, life carries on, even in the middle of the infamy in which it existed, it still survives.' In this context, art becomes the continuation of life. Indeed, in this piece I do not only see the memory of an oppressed existence, but that of an eternal presence. Beyond all that is factual, it is art that is the testimony of life.

Doris Salcedo
October 2002

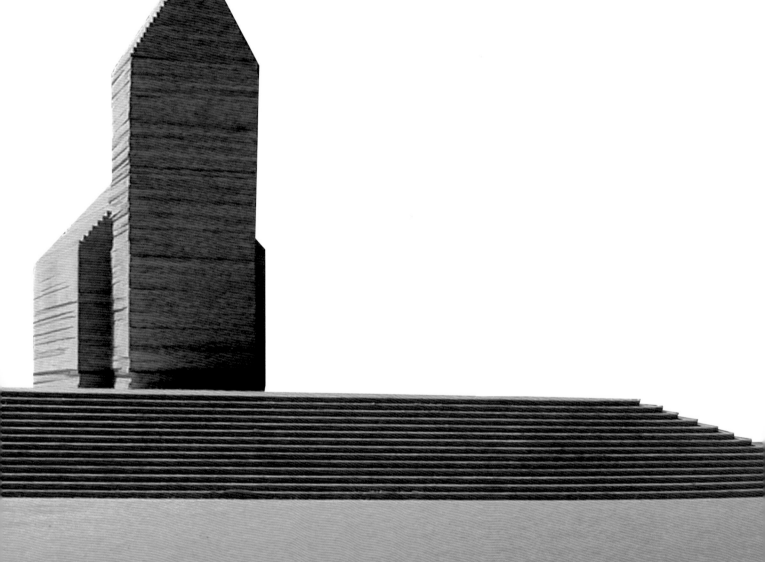

Proposal for a (unrealised) project for the Marsun Churchyard, Groningen, 2003

Nothing completely coincides, and everything intermingles or crosses over. Here the absolute is local, precisely because place is not delimited.
Deleuze and Guattari

This project is based on the idea that every single place or spot on earth has been contested, challenged or fought over at some point in history. While tangentially referring to the specific history of the Netherlands, my goal with this project is to establish a link to different events occurring all over the world, where fragile national identities and weak incipient states allow rampant violence to take place. While in some areas the conflict over the making of a place and the making of an identity are resolved, in others colonialism, forced displacement and deterritorialisation mark these landscapes as conflicted and uneasy.

Landscapes contain traces of past events, of memories and stories capable of establishing a relation between past and present. The Netherlands' landscape is no exception. The outbreak of the Reformation and the proliferation of protestant sects generated endless discussions and violent conflicts between those who tried to impose their own religious beliefs and those who defended their right to discern for themselves heterodoxically. These events played a key role in the consolidation of a national identity, and therefore led to the formation of a national state capable of revolting against King Philip II of Spain.

The Western view of landscapes creates a sense of things being in place, emphasises a panorama in which the observers stand back and distance themselves from the thing observed. We tend to engage in a contemplation of a vacuous landscape, devoid of meaning, as though we could not recognise the density and complexity of every single landscape. This limited idea of landscape has to be broadening if we want to understand the way people engage with their cultural and physical surroundings.

Therefore I propose to create a topography of war in the Marsun churchyard that will enable us to see this landscape in a more compelling way – not just as an inert landscape, but as the place where we face the emptiness and loss of all wars, historic and contemporary.

Doris Salcedo
April 2003

Proposal for a project for
the 8th International Istanbul
Biennial, 2003

The new piece I am proposing to make for the
8th International Istanbul Biennial will be a
topography of war, so deeply inscribed in
everyday life that, in spite of the fact that it
represents an extreme experience, the point
where normal conditions of life end and war
begins can no longer be clearly discerned. An
image where the private and the political collide,
producing a complete sense of disorientation.

I want to make a topographical piece, made up
of moments, fragments and relations. It will be
based on problems that arise from real historical
events, where opposing viewpoints violently
intersect, generating separation, discontinuity
and chaos. Emphasis will be placed on the
complex and difficult relations that emerge in
contested spaces or sites of war.

The presence of the subject in this piece will be
removed from inner psychological analysis,
to emphasise the context in which people
inhabiting contested spaces are caught up
and crossed by opposing forces that impose
transformations on their lives.

This piece intends to map spaces that are
disputed or struggled over. It will be made up of
several parts that conjoin and intersect with one
another, to the point where both logic and order
collapse. The piece will be devoid of a centre or
a climax, in order to focus attention on fissures,
on the small, the close-at-hand, and all the
apparently insignificant aspects of human life.

Doris Salcedo
April 2003

Proposal for a project for White Cube, London, 2004

W.G. Sebald poses a question about how to form a language in which terrible experiences, experiences capable of paralysing the power of articulation, could be expressed in art. I posed this question to myself when making this piece: how to find a way to address concentration camps – both historical ones and their contemporary versions? How to address the intolerable? Since I found no definitive answer to this question, I titled this piece *Neither*.

Neither is an indeterminate space, located beyond my powers to articulate, to understand and measure the political structure in which we live. *Neither* is a piece about uncertainty and ambiguity.

A piece that is simultaneously located outside and inside the epicentre of catastrophe, I strongly believe that *Neither* does not have to narrate any story, because the experience it is addressing is well known to all of us. It attests to the fact that there is no common frontier between what we see on our television screens and in our lives, and also to the fact that there *is* a common frontier between disenfranchised human beings and us.

For years I have kept files about concentration camps, historical ones as well as contemporary variations of the political structure that generate spaces where, as Hannah Arendt has said, 'Everything is possible.'

I am not only concerned with the atrocities that took place, and continue to take place, in such spaces, but focus my inquiry mainly on those aspects of our society that make possible the existence of spaces where absolutely inhumane conditions are accomplished. The concentration camp is not simply a terrible event produced by a sick society; it cannot be reduced to a German perversion. Concentration camps are the essential expression of the political structure of our time.

They have a long history that has come full circle: the first concentration camp was created by the Spaniards in Cuba in 1896, and now in Cuba we have Camp Delta in Guantanamo Bay. And in between, there is a terribly long list. The British, at the very beginning of the twentieth century, established concentration camps during the Boer Wars; in 1906 the Germans confined the entire Herero tribe, annihilating the majority of its members. Besides the German Lagers, there were the killing fields in Cambodia, the Soviet Gulags, camps for ethnic cleansing in the former Yugoslavia, Rwanda, Burundi, North Korea, people kidnapped in Colombia and kept for years in cages in the middle of the jungle, slave colonies in Istanbul, or on the island of Diego Garcia in the Indian Ocean … the list is endless.

With this piece I wanted to address the perverse ambiguity that characterises these spaces, where destitute human beings are included in territories that represent their absolute exclusion from society.

As Agamben writes, whoever enters a camp enters in a zone of absolute ambiguity and uncertainty. The interiority of these spaces are pure exteriority, in that the frontier between public and private is blurred. They are places established by law, but what happens inside them is nevertheless illegal: they have become a rule generated by exceptional laws. The brutal exclusion of concentration camps is thus included in our life.

Neither juxtaposes interiority with exteriority. It is an interior space that negates the possibility of interiority, of intimacy and remembrance.

Levinas has changed the Cartesian dictum 'I think therefore I am' to 'I dwell therefore I am'. To dwell is to exist. And he goes even further; for him to dwell is to be in a place where one is welcomed. Levinas equates the life of concentration-camp inmates to the existence of those shades Ulysses encounters in his descend to Hades.

Neither is a piece suspended in dead time. It attempts a rupture with historical time; it is not the present time built on continuous instances, but is rather an immobilised duration, and we experience it in the present tense only because we enter it. It is suspended in a dislocated time that breaks the thread of chronological order. In *Neither* background and foreground merge, and the gathering of memories is suspended. There is a radical silence, but a silence that I hope involves us in what is happening.

I wanted to disassociate my work from the way art has represented torture. Mostly it has been represented as a spectacle, as something we can watch. The implication is that it cannot be stopped, and the inactivity of the onlookers underscores this impotence.

I wanted *Neither* to be an experience. For this reason, there is nothing to be looked at, and we are there with no words to describe the intolerable.

Doris Salcedo
September 2004

Proposal for a project for the Triennial of Contemporary Art, Castello di Rivoli, Turin, 2005

The space of room 18 has an absolute character. The piece I am proposing to install in it emphasises both the form and the character of this grand space. It is not a distortion of it; it is rather a reinforcement of the specific aspects of the space.

I believe *Abyss* can help us trace the genesis of the space of room 18. It is a tool to decode or read the history and nature of this impressive and at times unapproachable space.

Room 18 is clearly a space of political practice, not a space of human habitation. The social practices inherent in the spatial form of this room remain present today, more than a century and a half after it ceased to be a centre of power.

Abyss addresses the sheer extra weight the powerful ones exert over disenfranchised populations. It is an attempt to address the irreconcilable disparity that prevails in the social practices of our time.

This piece is the result of long-term research into the fact that immigration has become nothing but a problem in the first world. Opinion polls show that there is consensus among the majority of the population in Europe and Australia, identifying immigrants as the perpetrators of an inexplicable wrong, as the source of all the problems they are enduring.

The rejection of immigrants as human beings, and the erasure of their status as political refugees or even as workers, makes evident the fact that they are the objects of a zealous hatred.

This general trend towards separatism, disintegration and racism is marked by the new space *Abyss* aims to delineate, a space that not only contains but also dominates the bodies it shelters.

Space is seen as a passive locus to be filled with objects – in the case of room 18, as a place to present paintings and sculptures. It is no more than an invisible backdrop that supports inanimate objects. This space remains invisible and without meaning.

The piece I am proposing will allow us to experience the complexity of this imposing space, as well as the ungraspable nature of its dome, located somewhere between a political hegemony and a transcendental idea.

Abyss intends to shows that space can play an active role in the construction of consciousness.

Doris Salcedo
June 2005

On 29 June 2007, eleven members of the
State Parliament of Valle in Colombia, were
assassinated. They had been kidnapped and
kept hostage by the guerrilla movement FARC
(Revolutionary Armed Forces of Colombia) since
11 April 2002. Immediately after hearing of their
assassination, I began organising an *Act of
Mourning* in the Plaza de Bolivar, the central
square of the city of Bogotá, which took place
on the 3 July. This *Act of Mourning* consisted of
filling the entire square with 24,000 candles in a
perfect grid. People from all around the city
came to help light the candles, which honoured
and commemorated, in a silent gesture, the
memory of these victims of violence.

Doris Salcedo
July 2007

Credits

Technical design of
Shibboleth **by the architects:**
Sergio Clavijo
Fredy Florez
Carlos Granada
Pia Mazzilli
Joaquín Sanabria